AND AFTER THIS?

And After This?

An Interpretation of the Christian Belief in Life after Death

by

THE REVEREND HARRY N. HANCOCK

*Rector of St. Thomas Episcopal Church
Bethel, Connecticut*

LONGMANS, GREEN AND CO.

NEW YORK   LONDON   TORONTO

LONGMANS, GREEN AND CO., INC.
55 FIFTH AVENUE, NEW YORK 3

LONGMANS, GREEN AND CO. Ltd.
6 & 7 CLIFFORD STREET, LONDON W 1

LONGMANS, GREEN AND CO.
20 CRANFIELD ROAD, TORONTO 13

AND AFTER THIS?
HARRY N. HANCOCK
COPYRIGHT · 1954

PUBLISHED SIMULTANEOUSLY IN THE DOMINION OF CANADA BY
LONGMANS, GREEN AND CO., TORONTO

FIRST EDITION

LIBRARY OF CONGRESS CATALOG CARD NUMBER 54-13146
Printed in the United States of America

FOREWORD

THE following pages make no claim to profound scholarship or originality of thought. They are simply an attempt to interpret to the ordinary man the Christian belief in eternal life.

The attempt was prompted by the growing realization that there are so many people, including many regular churchgoers, to whom such expressions as "the resurrection of the body" or "He descended into Hell" or "the Communion of Saints" are merely confusing and meaningless.

A student is always deeply indebted to good teachers and to the standard works of scholarship in his particular field of study. The present writer's debt will be obvious to any professional theologian who may chance to read these pages, and that debt is hereby gratefully acknowledged.

Numerous footnotes and references, other than to the Bible, are apt to scare away the very reader for whom this little treatise is intended, namely, the ordinary man who is interested and yet puzzled by the Christian belief in life beyond death. For the serious student, the scholar, and the theologian, there is no lack of larger, more specialized, and scholarly works.

CONTENTS

AND AFTER THIS?

CHAPTER I

INTRODUCTION

IT IS appointed unto men once to die." No one will question the truth of that statement. "But after this. . . ." What? This is a question which everyone has to face at least once in his lifetime. It is, in fact, a question of unfailing fascination, which is the

1

reason why mission preachers always draw their biggest congregations on the night when they are billed to preach about it, and why charlatans in spiritualism do such a roaring trade, especially in time of war. Yet for many years past this question has been seriously neglected by Christian preachers, the very people who ought to have something to say about it. I have asked many regular churchgoers whether they could remember when they last heard a sermon on the subject of life after death and, almost invariably, the answer was, "I can't remember a single one, except a few rather vague references to it at Easter."

The fact is that we are suffering from a hangover from the "Social Gospel" which was very much the fashion in our pulpits a generation ago. This has left us a dangerous legacy in the fact that Christianity is now so widely regarded simply as a code of social and personal ethics—very much a "this world" philosophy with a strong emphasis on what is popularly called "practical" Christianity, with a thick red line under "practical" to distinguish it from the phony theological and ecclesiastical stuff which, it is alleged, has been fooling humanity for the past two thousand years. This line of argument, as I well know from direct personal experience, is part of the technique adopted by those who seek to make converts to Communism from the Christian fringe, and many there are who fall for it. This accounts, at least in part, for the suspicion recently cast against protestant clergymen, that many of them are slightly pink around the edges.

There are, however, certain fundamental doctrines of the Christian Faith which distinguish it sharply and clearly even from the most academic Communism, and make the diametrical and irreconcilable opposition between the two unmistakably obvious. One of the most important is the Christian doctrine of eternal life, and neglect of it in the teaching and preaching of Christian pastors not only opens the way for the insidious infiltration of Communist doctrine under the guise of "practical" Christianity, but also leads to other results hardly less disastrous within the Christian community itself. For example, the extraordinary variety of ideas, hopes, fears, beliefs, and superstitions to be found even among the members of a single Christian congregation who have been worshipping God, listening to sermons, and saying their prayers and creeds together for twenty years or more, is quite astounding. Consequently, at times of mortal sickness and bereavement, when the pastor should be closest to his people, he finds, all too often, a great gulf between himself and them which he cannot cross; a kind of spiritual barrier due to the absence of a common language in which he might speak to them with any hope of being understood; and the inevitable grief of parting with loved ones made even worse by vague fears and confusion of thought, instead of being softened by that quiet confidence and dauntless hope which are the fruits of a reasonable faith. How often a minister is summoned to the bedside of a dying parishioner, only to be warned by the family before he enters the sickroom, that he must be very careful not to let the patient even suspect that he may be dying. "We just want you to try and cheer him up a bit." How often, too, the offer to bring the sacrament of Holy Communion to a patient in time of serious illness is refused with almost hysterical fear, even by people who are normally regular communicants. All this is symptomatic of a confusion of thought and lack of disciplined belief which rob the Christian Faith of its sustaining strength and power at the very time when they are needed most.

4

Such is the inevitable nemesis of catering to the popular demand for a creedless Christianity and an undisciplined and vague liberalism which reduces the New Testament conception of the Church as the Body of Christ to a society for the study of social ethics, and the Christian religion to a nebulous notion about doing good. We may indeed be grateful for all that the social implications of the Gospel have done for civilization; but a purely social gospel has little or nothing to say to the dying and the bereaved.

Belief in the life of the world to come, or the denial of that belief, exercises a profound, though often unconscious, influence upon our ordinary daily lives. One of the most popular, but mischievous, fallacies in which so many people take refuge from the necessity of thinking is the saying: "It doesn't matter what you believe, so long as you act right; it is not creeds that count, but conduct." That may be a comforting excuse for mental and spiritual laziness, but a little serious thought soon exposes the fallacy of it. The decisions we all have to make as we go through life— if we are normal, rational people—the particular course of action we choose in any given circumstances, is decided by our thinking. But our thinking

5

is, in turn, based upon our knowledge of the facts of the situation; and when definite knowledge is not available, as when we have to do with the future, then our decision must be based, not upon knowledge, but upon belief. It has to be, at least to some extent, an act of faith. We decide and act according to what we *believe* will be best for us. This is characteristic of what we call normal, rational behavior. Thus, a man's behavior will accord with what he believes about life and death. If a man really is convinced that physical death will be the final end of his existence, then the pattern of his behavior, his whole attitude toward life, is bound to be subtly different (I do not, for the moment, say better or worse—but *different*) from that of a man who is equally convinced that death will not be the end of him, but that after death must come judgment and, for better or for worse, eternal life.

Yet another reason for the vital importance of this question of belief in life after death is the fact that it is as true today as it was when the words were first written, that "if in this life only we have hope in Christ, we [Christians] are of all men most miserable," [1] that is, most to be pitied, because, like all

[1] I Cor. 15:9.

6

the millions of our predecessors in the Faith, we are gambling our precious three-score-years-and-ten on a pathetic illusion—and losing our bet! Our worship, our services and sacraments are a meaningless waste of time; our moral efforts and spiritual strivings are a mere chasing of shadows; our struggles with temptation a useless beating of the empty air; our funeral and memorial services a pathetic farce and the hope wherewith we seek to comfort the bereaved a cruel delusion. And above it all stands the cross of Christ as a monument to life's tragic futility. For, if crucifixion was indeed the end of the life of Christ, then His cross is simply a witness to the inevitable and eternal victory of death over life, of hatred over love, of the worst that men can do over the best that man can be. The story of His resurrection becomes the most hideous hoax that was ever perpetrated on mankind, and the Christian Church serves only to perpetuate the cruel deception. St. Paul put this in more restrained language when he wrote, "If Christ be not risen from the dead, then is our preaching vain, and your faith is also vain." [2]

And even if we allow the fullest weight to St.

[2] I Cor. 15:14.

7

Paul's influence on Christian theology, it still remains true that it is extremely difficult, to say the very least, to see how the clear teaching of Jesus Himself, as it is found in its purest and earliest known form in the very heart of the Gospels, can have any intelligible meaning whatsoever within the narrow limits of physical birth and death. What meaning, for example, can we give to all the parables of judgment and the parables of the Kingdom? If we take them as foretelling the establishment of an earthly paradise in this present world, then the whole weight of scientific knowledge in almost every field from biology to astronomical physics, not to mention the experience of the last two thousand years of human history, would seem to be dead against them. But even if, despite all this, there should be achieved at some far distantly future date on this planet, a state of affairs which could be truly described as an earthly paradise (including, perhaps, the Communist dream of a classless society!), even so, what conceivable significance, value or purpose could that have for all the countless millions of human souls who have, and will have, lived and struggled and suffered and perished long before that haunting dream is ever realized? "All

8

these," says the author of the Epistle to the Hebrews (almost certainly not St. Paul, by the way), "all these died in faith, not having received the promises." [3] All these, in other words, would seem to be no more than the waste material in the process of achieving perfect happiness for the few at the expense of the many. Such may be the ways of men. It is, as we have seen in our own lifetime, typical and characteristic of power politics and the megalomaniac dictator to be ruthlessly prodigal of human lives in sending millions to their deaths in order to protect the privileges of the few. But shall we dare to assume that this is also the way of God? If we do, then we come perilously close to the doctrine at the heart of that philosophy of life against which the Christian world is matching its strength today.

That is why we must face the fact that Christianity is not merely a code of morals. It is nothing if not a religion, and an "other worldly" religion at that. The founder of Christianity was concerned, and we must be too, not only with men's relations with one another, which is morality; but also with men's relations with God, which is religion. If eter-

[3] Hebrews 11:13.

9

nal life, as we learn of it in the New Testament, is not an actual reality, then the Christian religion is a snare and a delusion.

CHAPTER II

REASON

IN THE first and great commandment of the Law as summarized by Jesus Christ, we are bidden to love the Lord our God, not only with our hearts, which sometimes become a little overheated by our feelings, but also with our minds. We shall not be breaking the commandment if we begin our study of the Christian doctrine of life after death by trying to look at it first strictly in the light of reason. Our faith, if it is not to be mere superstition or blind credulity, must be reasonable faith. This does not mean that we shall believe only that which may be demonstrated like an experiment in physics or proved like a theorem in geometry. It means that we shall go as far in our search as the light of reason will take us, and then, from the point beyond which the leaden feet of logic will carry us no further, we shall rise on the wings of faith. But it will be a reasonable faith, based upon reasonable grounds for belief.

First then, let us consider the unquestionable facts at our disposal and see what we can reasonably deduce from them. The first fact which we can surely accept without question is the fact of our own existence. "I think, therefore I am." But a stone also exists, even though it does not think. Both a stone and a man are material objects which occupy space and are subject to the force of gravity. Yet no one will question the fact that there is a vast difference between a stone and a man. What, exactly, is the

12

difference? This is not as easy a question to answer as it might appear, and we shall find it easier to illustrate than to define. Perhaps the best illustration for our present purpose is to point out that, while the stone exists only in one way, as an object which the man can see and feel, i.e., *objectively*, the man, on the other hand, exists in two ways. He exists, like the stone, as an object which other men can see and touch; but, unlike the stone, he also exists as a subject who in turn perceives, is aware of, can see and touch other people, i.e., *subjectively*. It is important to get this distinction clear. What we are aware of objectively is what goes on *outside* ourselves, and this awareness can be shared by other people. Two or three men can be aware of one stone in their path. What we are aware of subjectively is what goes on *inside* ourselves, and this is something which no other human being can share. The poet, the painter, the sculptor, and perhaps especially, the musician try to share this kind of subjective experience through the medium of their art; but they never quite succeed. We can never be quite sure (because we have no means of knowing) that the feelings, the emotional experiences which their poems, paintings, and music arouse in us are the

13

same as those which, in them, inspired the particular work of art. There are heights and depths of spiritual and emotional experience in your life and mine which no other human being, even our nearest and dearest, can fully share. The reason is that such experiences are subjective. They belong to us and to us alone. This is what makes us individuals.

There are, then, two distinct ways in which I, as a human individual, exist. I exist as an object which other people can see and touch and recognize as part of their environment. For the people who meet me on the street I am, so to speak, part of the scenery or an obstacle to be avoided. Incidentally, I can only exist in this way (objectively) so long as there is someone else, a perceiving person, to be aware of me. But even if I am alone in the middle of a desert or an ocean, with no other living being within many miles and entirely outside the range of anyone else's awareness of my existence, nevertheless I still "am." I still have my own being, my own thoughts, feelings, memories, and emotions. I am still aware of myself and of my environment. In a word, I can still exist *subjectively* whether any other human being in this world is aware of my existence or not.

14

With this in mind, let us consider a second fact which we can surely accept without question, namely, the fact of death. Sooner or later, by disease, violence, or sheer senility, we shall die. Have you ever wondered what it feels like to die? That question is by no means as silly as it may sound. How often we hear someone say in the course of a conversation, "I felt as if I were dying." Actually, however, no living person has even the vaguest notion of what it feels like to die. The only ideas we have about it are those we may have gained from watching someone else die, and observing the physical signs which accompany the process, such as absence of pulse, cessation of respiration, loss of temperature, the onset of rigor mortis, and so forth. There are times when it takes the expert knowledge of the physician to decide whether a person is actually dead or in a state of deep coma or catalepsy. The point is that we can only see death *from the outside*, which means objectively. We can no more share another person's experience of dying than we can feel another person's pain. A sufferer may try to describe his pain to us by likening it to some common experience such as the sensation of a sharp stab or burn. But the person who dies cannot give us any

15

such description of his experience. And even if he could, our knowledge would, at best, be second-hand, hearsay rather than evidence.

All we can ever know about death, therefore, is something of what it does to other people's bodies; and we may draw the obvious conclusion that it will someday do the same to our own. Even then, however, it is seriously questionable whether we shall ever really know just what it means to die, any more than we know what it means to be sound asleep. We only know what it feels like to be very sleepy; and we only know that so long as we are not yet quite asleep. We do not realize that we have been asleep until we are, at least partially, awake again. That mysterious hinterland of unconsciousness, in which all feeling, thought and memory are dissolved in the complete oblivion we call sleep, is a familiar phenomenon; but we can give no more account of it subjectively than we can of death itself. And if death is indeed "a deep and dreamless sleep from which there is no awakening" then we shall not experience it any more than the patient, deep in anesthesia on the operating table, experiences the sharp incision of the scalpel and the movement of the surgeon's fingers; for in that case to die means to pass

16

from a condition of feeling, awareness, and consciousness (however dim), into a condition of not feeling or knowing anything at all, of complete unawareness and unconsciousness. Obviously, however, we cannot feel that we are not feeling anything; we cannot experience the total absence of experience. Therefore we cannot experience the change from one state to the other, which, on the view we have been supposing, is death.

We may, if we choose, believe that death is just this—the transition from a state of awareness, thought, feeling, memory, and self-consciousness into the blank oblivion of utter nothingness and non-existence. Many people prefer to believe this rather than the Christian doctrine of life beyond physical death. But they can only *believe* and *hope* that this is so. They can no more demonstrate or prove it than the Christian can demonstrate or prove his belief in the life of the world to come. The plain fact is that there is no logical reason whatsoever for *assuming* that the mysterious and vital part of us which makes the difference between a living personality and a corpse has necessarily ceased to exist or to have any further experiences of its own, simply because the means of its communication with us, the physical body, has broken down beyond repair and must be discarded. For all we can tell from the outside (where we must remain as spectators until our own turn comes to die), the soul, spirit, ego, personality, or whatever we choose to call it, may be more alive than ever in another state of life.

The first step, then, that reason takes us is a small one, but a vitally important one; namely, that there is no rational ground for *assuming* (without the slightest proof) that life beyond physical death is impossible. The Christian's belief in eternal life, therefore, is not against reason. But this does not carry us very far. It shows that we are moving in the right direction; but, if our belief in eternal life is to be real and strong, it is scarcely enough merely to know that it is not irrational. Let us see, then, if we can go a step further.

A third fact which, I think, we can accept as true without argument is that, in the comparatively brief period of time between birth and death, there is no recognizable relation that we can discover between goodness and happiness, between righteousness and prosperity; no dependable scale or standard whereby virtue is rewarded and wickedness is punished.

18

We all know quite well how often the finest characters are the greatest sufferers, and how the wicked
flourish and prosper—so often, indeed, that it sometimes seems to be the rule rather than the exception.
Such things as cancer and polio, bombs and airline
disasters do not distinguish between the righteous
and the unrighteous, between the just and the un-
just. They both perish alike and come to the same
end. And so, between birth and death—both of
which are beyond our own volition, for we did not
ask to be born and we cannot choose but die—between these two events we live our little day in what
seems to be a confused medley of pleasure and pain,
sorrow and joy, success and failure, good and evil,
beauty and ugliness; a state of confusion that has no
law but blind chance and meaningless accident!

The interesting question is this. Why do we feel
(as we all do) that there *ought* to be any law, any
relation between integrity and happiness, righteousness and prosperity? Why should we feel, as the
Psalmist did twenty-five hundred years ago, any
wonder or resentment at the sufferings of the inno-
cent and the prosperity of the wicked? Is there, after
all, any reason why righteousness *should* be re-

warded and evil-doing punished? Why should we feel badly, and sometimes very bitter and resentful, when we see a really fine person suffering and dying in slow agony, while a vicious blackguard lives heartily to be ninety and dies peacefully in his sleep? There is no denying that, quite regardless of religion, we all feel a strong sense of injustice, even immorality, about such things. We feel that someone, whom we must call God if only for lack of another name, must be to blame. But why?

The answer is that these things offend our sense of justice, our instinctive and insistent demand for rationality. After all, the outstanding characteristic of the world around us is its order, its reasonableness, its breath-taking precision in everything from microbes to the Milky Way; the invariable fixity of its laws and the unfailing orderliness and intelligent design of it all. This is something we feel we can depend on. The whole vast superstructure of modern science does, in fact, depend on just this belief that the universe is rational and governed by fixed laws. And we feel, with a deep-rooted instinct, that it is *right* that this should be so. Surely it is not unreasonable, therefore, to expect that the most wonderful thing in such a world, human personality, should also be rational, should also have order, rationality, significance, and a purpose to be achieved.

If, however, the mysterious phenomenon we call death is really the final end and extinction of human life, then certain conclusions necessarily follow. It follows not only that the saint and the blackguard perish alike without difference or distinction, but also that the age-long struggle of a thousand generations of men and women from primitive beginnings to the mastery of life we know today, a struggle in which every step of progress is marked with blood and sacrifice, toil and tears, is all foredoomed to end in dust and ashes. In this view man is just a biological or evolutionary accident, a rather lost and frightened creature in a universe teeming with terrific forces which seem bent on his destruction. If human life is just a brief flicker of more or less painful self-consciousness, which sparks into life only to be snuffed out again in the surrounding darkness, then human history, with what we regard as its glorious achivements, is just a momentary mess on a tiny fragment of matter whirling aimlessly in unimaginable infinity; and humanity's ultimate destiny is nothing but the tomb of a cold and lifeless universe.

What then becomes of all our endless talk of justice, freedom, truth, the dignity of human personality, and all the rest of such highfalutin nonsense? It is as the buzzing of a fly upon the windowpane—as swiftly ended and with as little significance in the scheme of things.

There are, of course, many people who accept this view of human life and destiny because they cannot feel that the evidence for anything in the nature of life beyond physical death is strong enough to convince them of its truth. Others reject what they imagine is the Christian belief in eternal life because they are repelled by the idea of golden streets above the bright blue sky and horrified at the prospect of an unending symphony for strings and chorus! Still others, who cannot plead the honest doubts of intellectual integrity, ignore rather than reject, the Christian belief because they have never grown up. They are like young children for whom life is just one minute long—this minute. They never exercise the ability, which man alone possesses, to "look before and after and pine for what is not." But we cannot remain children forever. Sooner or later the question will force itself upon us and demand an answer. For my own part, I simply cannot believe that a human personality, which is the most wonderful thing within our knowledge, is the only mad and meaningless thing in an otherwise rational and orderly world. Nor can I believe that the instinctive reverence for human personality and respect for the inherent rights of the individual, which are characteristic of the best and noblest achievements of civilization, are based on nothing more than a pathetic illusion.

If the life span of the individual human person is, at most, seventy or eighty years which lead only to annihilation, then it may be possible to argue that he is of very little importance apart from his value to the state or nation, which may last for a thousand years. This, in effect, is precisely what the materialist philosophy of Communism does say. But if the Christian belief is true, then the thousand years which the state may last (though precious few of them do!) is as nothing in comparison with the eternal life and destiny of the individual. Totalitarianism thinks only in terms of the herd; Christianity thinks in terms of the precious individual. This is the major issue that confronts the world today. Only if

23

the Christian belief in eternal life is false can the philosophy of totalitarianism be true.

We conclude, therefore, on what we claim to be entirely rational grounds, and with the support of such evidence as is available, that physical death is neither the end nor the purpose of human life; but that human destiny, both individual and corporate, far transcends its history and is the complete and perfect fulfilment of it.

CHAPTER III

REASONABLE FAITH

IN THE last chapter we reached the conclusion
that there is no strictly rational ground for assuming
that physical death is *necessarily* the final end of a
human life, that there is no logical, much less demonstrable, reason why life beyond the death of the

body should be impossible. This does not seem to take us very far; but at least it leaves the way open and that in itself is important because it means that in believing in eternal life Christians are not, as some would say, flying in the face of reason and trying to believe something which is manifestly absurd. Unless we are prepared to admit that human life and history constitute the one utterly meaningless muddle in an otherwise perfectly ordered and orderly universe, whose chief characteristic is intelligent and purposive design, then it would seem that such evidence as is available is more in favor of Christian faith than against it.

Let us now try to go a step further. If we grant that life after death is at least a possibility, the next question that naturally arises is: What kind of life? This is a question on which imagination has run riot, with very unhappy results. We must, therefore, approach it with restraint and care. We must try to distinguish what the late Professor A. E. Taylor of Edinburgh calls "our natural and reasonable anticipations" [1] from that which is mere fanciful imagining without any rational justification whatsoever.

One of the things of which we are most acutely

[1] A. E. Taylor, *Christian Hope of Immortality* (London: Geoffrey Bles, 1938).

conscious, at any rate in our more thoughtful moments, is a disturbing sense of life's incompleteness. A lifetime of study only leaves us more aware of the depths of our ignorance; years of patient research can barely touch the fringe of nature's garment; always there is something just beyond our grasp, something which, even in the longest life, there will not be time to do. Goodness, truth, and beauty seem to remain tantalizingly beyond the grasp of saint, scientist, and artist alike; and even the humblest of us is haunted by dreams and hopes and aspirations which ever elude complete fulfilment and satisfaction. Man cannot long for that which has no existence. A man dying of thirst in the desert may believe you if you tell him you have no water to give him: he will not believe you if you tell him that no such thing as water exists. His thirst convinces him beyond all argument. It seems reasonable, therefore, to expect that, if eternal life means anything at all, it means the eventual completion, fulfilment, and satisfaction of what we now know and possess only in part; above all, the fulfilment and perfection of personality, fully aware of itself and free from all the weaknesses and imperfections which spoil it now.

But human personality can scarcely exist (indeed it is questionable whether it can exist at all), much less be developed and preserved, except by constant intercourse and communion with other personalities. It is this capacity to reach out and communicate with others that gives to human personality its essential character. Another reasonable anticipation about the life of the world to come, therefore, is that it will be the life of a society of persons—individual personalities, not less but better able to recognize and enter into communion with one another than they are now. We shall have occasion to refer to this point later.

There is one characteristic feature of human life which, perhaps more than any other, distinguishes it from the life of the animal kingdom and gives to human personality its dignity and value. This is our freedom to exercise intelligent choice and our consequent sense of what we call moral responsibility. There have been attempts to deny the reality of human free will and to affirm that human behavior is completely and chemically predetermined by such things as our genes and chromosomes, or even by the way our mothers bathed and nursed us. The fact remains, however, that we all live, from day to day, on the unquestioned assumption that we are, in fact, free agents; and our society is ordered and governed on the principle that men and women are morally responsible for their behavior. Those who are obviously not receive special treatment, for their own benefit and for the protection of society at large. Whether such treatment is that of penology or psychology, or both, makes no difference to the argument. It also seems reasonable to expect, therefore, that free will and moral responsibility will not be without their effect upon the life of the world to come. It is obvious enough that, in this present life, a man's achievement of personality depends to a large extent upon his moral efforts and use of opportunities. Unless our free will and sense of moral responsibility are indeed the merest delusions, it must be possible to "work out our own salvation" and also possible to fail, or even refuse, to do so.

Yet another reasonable anticipation is that, just as such qualities as goodness, courage, nobility, humility, and strength of character are entirely independent of birth, race, wealth, environment, or education, so also eternal life will not be the special prerogative of any particular group or class, but an opportunity equally open to all men in virtue of their common humanity.

To sum up: It seems reasonable to expect that the gift of eternal life will mean a life of fulfilment and completion; a life of communion and intercourse between self-conscious personalities; a life which is open to all men in virtue of their humanity; and yet a heritage which, as a necessary consequence of our free will and moral responsibility, we may either grasp or cast away.

So far we have made no appeal at all to Holy Scripture because we have been trying to see how far in our search for the truth we could travel on the basis of logical reasoning and experience of life as we know it now. Let us now compare these "natural and reasonable anticipations" with the teaching of the New Testament. We said first that eternal life means fulfilment and completion. "I am come," said Jesus, "that they might have life, and that they might have it more abundantly." [2] "And this is life eternal, that they might know thee the only true God, and Jesus Christ, whom thou hast sent." [3] "For now," says St. Paul, "we see through a glass, darkly; but then face to face: now I know in part; but then shall I

[2] John 10:10.   [3] John 17:3.

30

know even as also I am known." [4] It is in such affirmations as these that we have the real essence of the New Testament teaching on eternal life, which consists, above all, in knowing God, the ultimate source of all goodness, truth, and beauty. For the majority of people who have no deep and real religious conviction, the primary interest in the life of the world to come is the possibility of reunion with loved ones from whom they have been parted by death. This is no more than natural, especially at the time of bereavement. But Christianity insists in putting God at the center. The reward of the pure in heart is to see God, in whom all the longings, searchings, strivings, and yearnings of the human heart find their perfect and complete fulfilment. "It doth not yet appear what we shall be: but we know . . . we shall be like him; for we shall see him as he is." [5] Even the Psalmist, centuries before, could say, "As for me, I shall behold thy face in righteousness; when I awake, I shall be satisfied with beholding thy form." [6] But, while the Christian Faith certainly puts God at the center of life, both here and for eternity, there is nothing in the Christian doctrine

[4] I Cor. 13:12.
[5] I John 3:2.
[6] Psalms 17:15. (Revised Standard Version)

31

of the life of the world to come which is comparable with the Buddhist Nirvana; there is no suggestion of the human soul losing its individuality by being swallowed up in the being of God.

This brings us naturally to our second "reasonable anticipation"— that the life of the world to come will be a life of communion in a society of personalities. In this connection, the words of Jesus to the penitent thief on the cross are significant. "Verily I say unto thee, Today shalt thou be with me in paradise." [7] The use of the personal pronouns is important. Both Jesus and the thief were about to die and they were both well aware of it; yet, if the words of Jesus mean anything at all, they mean that the "I" and the "thee" this side of death will persist in the "thou" and the "me" on the other side. Whatever meaning we may give to the word paradise in this context, it is evidently, in the mind of Christ, a condition of life in which "I" shall still be I and "you" will still be you, distinct personalities capable of recognition and communion.

Our third reasonable anticipation—that eternal life is open to all men in virtue of their common humanity—finds its confirmation in the New Testament by

[7] Luke 23:43.

the fact that there is no trace anywhere of the idea
that God's gift of a full and complete personality is
restricted to any select few. Christ's own word is
whosoever: . . . "whosoever liveth and believeth in
me." [8] From time to time, however, men have at-
tempted to impose conditions of their own making
on God's gift of eternal life, and our folly in this respect has driven us to opposite extremes. On the one
hand, there is the notion that salvation can only be
obtained (and somewhat mechanically, at that,
with the minimum of moral effort!) by joining a particular church. On the other hand, in a natural reaction against such stupid pride, we find the idea that
religion is an entirely private affair between the individual soul and God. The truth, as always, is to be
found between the extremes. Salvation, according
to the New Testament, certainly depends on a *personal* relation between the individual soul and God;
but this relation is by no means a *private* one. "Fellowship" is one of the great keywords of the New
Testament and "the fellowship of Christ's religion"
is of the very essence of Christianity, for it is the
only atmosphere in which personality can live and
breathe.

[8] John 11:26.

Yet eternal life, although it is the free gift of God to all who will accept it, is nevertheless a heritage which, by virtue of our free will and moral responsibility, we may either grasp and hold fast or else cast away. This is not only confirmed but heavily underlined in the teaching of Jesus himself. In parable after parable He shows that the precious gift of eternal life may be rejected or lost by our own wilfulness or carelessness. It is very easy to sentimentalize about Heaven, and the Christian doctrine of eternal life has suffered a great deal from it in popular thought. Such misconceptions as those contained, for example, in the jingle about "Pie in the sky, up on high, when you die," and the implication that mansions in Heaven are a kind of compensation (strictly pro rata!) for slums on earth, are utterly foreign to the whole spirit and meaning of the New Testament. There is, in fact, an aspect of the Christian doctrine of life after death and the destiny of man which is far from comfortable and soothing. We shall consider this in a later chapter on the doctrine of judgment.

Meanwhile, if what we have said so far is anywhere near the truth, then we may claim for the Christian doctrine of eternal life at least this much: rightly understood, it is not just a sentimental piece of wishful thinking. In the very nature of the case it is incapable of demonstration; but it conforms with and confirms those "reasonable anticipations" which are independently available to all of us as thinking rational beings. And so we move on, as we must, from reason to faith, from direct knowledge to belief, hope, and trust. But it is a confident hope because it is founded upon a reasonable faith.

CHAPTER IV

RESURRECTION
OF THE BODY

So FAR we have been thinking in more or less general terms; but now we must consider the specifically Christian belief about eternal life, which, as we might expect, has certain definite features peculiar to itself. It is with these that we shall be concerned from this point on.

It is typical of advancing civilization, with its increasing knowledge of the world around us, its scientific development and control over natural forces, that it always tends to purge away ancient beliefs which were universally held in man's primeval infancy. As the scope of man's knowledge widens and enlarges, fetishes, taboos, and superstitions gradually disappear. From time to time there are, of course, temporary lapses and setbacks, as for example, with the Christian religion itself during the Dark Ages. But this was corrected in due course by the revival of learning and the consequent Reformation. Nor are such lapses confined to what we call the Dark Ages. This enlightened twentieth century, as we used to call it, has some pretty ugly spots to show to posterity! The point is, however, that we recognize these lapses for what they are, and, on the whole, our movement is upward and onward. In view of this, it is a thought-provoking fact that belief in life after death, which is as primitive and universal as anything in human history, so far from being purged away by advancing knowledge and discarded (like witchcraft, black magic, and polytheism), has, in fact, become clearer, more definite, and stronger with the passing centuries. We can trace a tremendous development in this belief from its earliest form in the dawn of human history, through the Old Testament and up to the great spiritual heights reached, for example, in the Apologia of Socrates in the great days of Greek philosophy and science. What began as a primitive instinct seems to have kept pace with man's moral, spiritual, and intellectual growth. But with Christianity comes the greatest change of all. The emphasis is entirely shifted. The ancient Greeks believed in the immortality of the human soul, but, for them, the hereafter was a kind of dim underworld peopled by pale ghosts who were mere shadows of their former selves and living in a perpetual gloom of semidarkness. Obviously, such a life was a very poor second best by comparison with life in this present world.

But in the Christian Faith everything is seen from the viewpoint of eternity. This does not mean that Christianity in any way belittles the value or importance of this earthly life, as some of our more sentimental hymns might suggest. The Christian is no more anxious to "shuffle off this mortal coil" than anyone else. Indeed, the Christian Church in its very early days had to discourage the tendency of many of her members to rush too eagerly to martyrdom, and she still regards the deliberate ending of this life by suicide as a deadly sin, unless the unfortunate person concerned was "of unsound mind" and therefore not morally responsible. (This is why such phrases as "while the balance of his mind was disturbed" came to be added to the verdict of suicide in coroners' courts, in order that the victims might receive Christian burial with the rites of the Church.) The truth is that the Christian religion regards this present life, despite its brevity, as infinitely important: but it is important, not so much for its own sake as because it is the beginning, the one way of approach, to what lies beyond. And what lies beyond, in the Christian belief, is not a poor and paler reproduction or continuation of this present life, but a richer, fuller, and complete achievement of personality. The Christian hope is of life, not less, but more abundant. This, very briefly, is what is meant by saying that while Greek philosophy taught the immortality of the soul, the Christian religion teaches the resurrection of the body.

At this point we must pause to consider what is meant by the "resurrection of the body." The clause in the Apostles' Creed which uses these words, "I believe in the resurrection of the body" has often been interpreted in a misguided and materialistic fashion which has caused many sincere and genuinely thoughtful people to reject it as absurd and impossible. Others who still repeat the words every time they say the Creed, find them meaningless and confusing. What then does this clause mean? To put it in a sentence, it means that, ultimately, we shall lose nothing by death. But we must examine it a little more closely. The little time and patience this will demand will be well spent if it helps us to get rid of mistaken and misleading ideas on this subject.

It is a fact which few would challenge that the body is a real and essential part of us. It is the indispensable medium of our self-expression. But we can think of the human body in at least two entirely different ways, even though, in English, we have only one word to carry both meanings. For example, from

40

the specialized viewpoint of the pathologist or bio-chemist, a human body is a hundred and fifty pounds or so of chemicals, mostly iron, salt, and water. But that is not at all how we normally think of the human body, especially the body of someone we love. To us it is, above all, the medium of communication and communion between personalities; between all that is meant by "you" and "I." It happens that this medium of communion between living, spiritual beings consists, in this world, of what we call matter, something we can see and handle. We cannot think without a brain, or speak without tongue, lips and larynx, or act without hands and feet, all of which are solid, material things. We just cannot imagine what we should be like without a body. A disembodied spirit is actually inconceivable to the human mind. We cannot think of it without giving it some kind of shape or form, even if it be only a floating mist or a flapping sheet! A disembodied spirit, whatever it may be, is certainly something less than a whole and complete person. Yet we know, beyond any shadow of doubt, that the immediate result of the physical phenomenon we call death is that this body of our flesh is made not only useless

41

and incapable of any further communication, but even objectionable, so that we have to bury or burn it. "Earth to earth, ashes to ashes, dust to dust." And that, so far as we can see, is the end of the most wonderful creation in the world.

Yet, in spite of all this, the Christian Faith confidently affirms that death will not finally rob us of anything worth keeping, anything essential to a whole and complete personality. Now this is obviously a much bigger and more difficult conception than the Greek belief in the immortality of the soul; and, in order to try to get this difference as clear as we can, we must go slowly and take one step at a time. First, the Christian belief in eternal life does not mean a mere *continuity* of existence. That is why we have carefully avoided the phrase "everlasting life" which is so easily misunderstood. There is much more than that in the Christian hope. Second, even if we could prove that the soul does survive the death of the body and goes on living "by itself" so to speak, that would not necessarily mean that it will go on living forever. The soul might perish some time, long or short, after the death of the body. Third, it is quite possible to believe in the immortality of the soul as a survivor from the wreck of death, without believing in God at all. It is equally possible to believe in God and to deny the immortality of the soul. Many people do. This kind of immortality is, in fact, a more suitable field of study for what is called Psychical Research than for religion. The Christian religion is concerned not merely with the soul's possible survival of the accident of death, but with the redemption and salvation of the whole man, and the fulfilment of the destiny for which he was created—to become the friend of God. We must never forget that the Christian doctrine of eternal life is centered and anchored in our belief and trust in God; and in this connection there are two truths, commonly overlooked, which we must point out.

The first concerns the common assumption that spirit and matter, soul and body, are eternally distinct and separate and eternally in conflict. But this is nothing more than an assumption and is no part of Christian Faith. God created man's body as well as his soul, and, as we shall see later, the mysterious connection between the spiritual and the material is life's most baffling reality. But it is an undeniable reality. The second truth is that the victory which the Christian Faith claims to have been won by Jesus Christ on Calvary was not a victory *over* death, but a victory *through, by means of* death. Jesus did not escape from death. He died. Between Good Friday evening and Easter morning, the Son of God was dead; as dead as you and I will some day be. The Apostles' Creed insists, with pounding hammer-blows of emphasis, that "He was crucified, dead, and buried." Dr. Oliver Quick explains this in a fine passage in his *Doctrines of the Creed* thus:

"Christianity, alone among the religions and philosophies of the world, succeeds in eliciting from death, i.e., from the actuality of dying, a unique value, so that it is found to make a positive and necessary contribution to the perfection of created life. Other philosophies of immortality suggest either that death is in some way unreal, or that it constitutes merely a release for the spirit through the dropping off of the material body. Not so Christianity. To it dying is an essential part or moment in that act through which love accomplishes the self-sacrifice which issues in eternal life. And thus physical death, in all its terrible universality, becomes for the Christian a sacrament of the spiritual truth that, because it is love which saves, life must be lost before it can be fully won." [1]

[1] Oliver Quick, *Doctrines of the Creed* (London: James Nisbet & Co., Ltd., 1938), p. 213.

And it was Jesus Himself who said, "Except a corn of wheat fall into the ground and die, it abideth alone: but if it die it bringeth forth much fruit." [2]

Now the guarantee of the victory won by Jesus Christ through death is His resurrection; and this, in turn, is the basis of the Christian belief in the resurrection of the body rather than in the immortality of the soul, and the Church has been led to formulate her beliefs by the appearances of the risen Lord after His resurrection. A detailed discussion of the evidence for the resurrection of Jesus Christ from the dead is beyond the scope of these pages; but it is of such vital importance that we must at least state some of the salient points.

To begin with we must realize that the preaching of the resurrection of Jesus Christ from the dead by the first apostles was news and not, as it is now, history. They were speaking of an event which had happened, not thousands of miles away and nearly two thousand years ago, but right there in the city where they were preaching and only a few weeks before. Moreover there were many people listening to them who had actually seen the crucifixion, and the tomb in Joseph's garden was within walking

[2] John 12:24.

45

distance. Time and familiarity had not bred indifference or reduced the question to one of merely academic interest. To use a contemporary idiom, the preaching of the apostles would have "made the headlines." It is clear, therefore, that those apostles must have been mightily convincing and able to produce some weighty evidence in order to persuade, as they did, so many of their hearers of the truth of their astounding claim that this Jesus, who had been crucified, dead and buried, was alive, and that they had seen and spoken with Him many times. For our present purpose it will be sufficient to refer to three facts on which the apostles' deep conviction was founded.

First, there was the empty tomb. The fact that the tomb was empty on the third morning has never been successfully challenged. The most that sceptical critics have been able to do is to suggest alternative explanations for the fact. Some of these suggestions are interesting; but they all raise more problems than they solve and they show how far ingenuity will go in trying to avoid the one explanation which the critic has already determined, on other grounds, to reject. It has been suggested, for example, that the Jews removed the body of Jesus from the tomb by order of the Sanhedrin. If this were true, then the Jews had only to produce the body and the resurrection would have immediately become an exploded myth. The Sanhedrin would certainly have done this if it had been at all possible. It has also been suggested that the Roman soldiers removed the body from the tomb. If this had been the case, it would have been the easiest thing in the world for Pontius Pilate to nip Christianity in the bud by exposing it as a hideous fraud as soon as the preaching of the resurrection began. Pilate would have given a good deal to be able to do just that. If he had been able to destroy Christianity at birth, so to speak, by producing the dead body of Jesus, why did he not do so?

Another suggestion, which is found, at any rate as a suspected possibility, in the gospel narrative itself, is that the apostles themselves might have removed the body of Jesus from the tomb. It was in order to prevent this that the military guard was posted. But if, in spite of this precaution, the apostles did somehow succeed in removing (and concealing without a trace!) the body of Jesus, this would make them deliberate liars and parties to a most heartless hoax. But even if this were true, we are still faced

47

with the question, why should they have persisted in a fraud which, so far from bringing them any kind of gain or advantage, only brought them danger, persecution, and frequently, a horrible death? We know that men will die, and die bravely and willingly, for what they believe to be the truth, even though subsequent events may prove that they were, in fact, mistaken. They will not die willingly for something which they themselves know, better than anyone else, and beyond all shadow of doubt, to be false. And besides all this, the deliberate perpetration of such a deception by the apostles is utterly inconsistent with all that we know of their lives and characters. Yet another suggested explanation of the empty tomb, attributed to the Jewish scholar Klausner, is known as "The Swoon Theory." This suggests that Jesus did not actually die on the cross, but fell into a deep state of coma or catalepsy, which is quite easily mistaken for death; and then, in the cool interior of the rock tomb, revived and made his escape, possibly with the help of some of the apostles. This would make, not only the apostles, but Jesus Himself a deliberate liar and deceiver. But, even so, what became of Jesus after He recovered? Where did He live and eventually die, without leaving the slightest trace? The fact is that no other explanation of the empty tomb has ever been found to fit all the facts; and every suggested alternative to the preaching of the first apostles has been found to raise more difficulties than it solves.

The second fact on which the conviction of the apostles was founded was the appearance of the risen Christ to them at various times and places. Many books have been written on this subject alone, and the reader who wishes to go further into it will have no difficulty in finding them. Here it must suffice to mention a few of the more popular objections and criticisms. It is pointed out, for example, that there are discrepancies between the various accounts of the resurrection appearances in the gospels: but this is testimony to their transparent sincerity and substantial accuracy. Independent witnesses of almost any event will show similar differences in their recollected accounts of it, unless there has been collusion. Lack of any discrepancies would be much graver cause for suspicion. Indeed it has been said that if ever a book on the history of testimony should be well and authoritatively written, the apostles of Jesus would rank very near the top of a list of the world's most reliable and accurate witnesses. They were what we should call "ordinary" men; neither exceptionally stupid nor exceptionally brilliant; neither particularly pious nor particularly evil or vicious. For the most part they were men who lived an open-air life and were healthy both in mind and body. Moreover, they were obviously men of independent spirit, sufficiently so to be divided among themselves in their opinions. They were not drawn from the ranks of the wealthy; but neither were they from the poorest in the land. Poverty is apt to destroy independence of mind and spirit. They were, in fact, exactly the kind of men who might be expected to see the heart of a matter and give a true verdict.

It has also been suggested that the alleged appearances of Jesus to the apostles were mere hallucinations. This, however, is psychologically unsound because hallucination presupposes expectation, and, so far from expecting any such thing, they were, as they readily admit, scared half out of their wits when Jesus appeared to them for the first time. They themselves were hard to convince and were inclined to dismiss the whole thing as the "idle tales" of hysterical women. Nowadays the most popular explanation of the resurrection appearances is to regard them as a kind of "spiritual truth" revealed to the apostles in visions; but we know of no preaching of the resurrection in apostolic days which did not include the raising and transforming of the Lord's body. If there was, in fact, no real resurrection, then we have to account for the mysterious and complete disappearance of the crucified body. It is, of course, quite possible for people born into a family and a society which has been steeped for centuries in the Christian tradition to reject the idea of Christ's resurrection from the dead, and yet retain their belief in Him as their living savior. But this is not the point at issue. The real question is: could those first apostles ever have achieved such a faith in the first place, if Christ's body had remained in the grave?

The third foundation of the apostles' deep conviction was their own living experience. The difference between the men who, in the Garden of Gethsemane, forsook Him and fled, and those who, a few weeks later could not be quelled or intimidated by prison, torture or death, is obvious enough to need no underlining. They were the same men. But something had happened which changed them completely. They themselves were so very sure that they knew what had caused this change that they suffered torture and death rather than deny it. And their experience has been perpetuated down the centuries in the Christian Church. On the first Good Friday evening, about the year A.D. 29, Jesus of Nazareth lay dead and buried, his crucified body in a sealed and guarded tomb. He died a failure. Even the few who, up till then, still believed in Him, had scattered and fled. No word of His teaching had been recorded. Yet within a few weeks a new movement, founded on the conviction that He had risen from dead, began to spread and win converts. Over three hundred years of cruel and bloody persecution failed to stamp it out and, against fantastically impossible odds, it not only survived but conquered. This is *the* miracle of history. And today, nearly two thousand years afterwards, millions of men and women of every nation under heaven, from the richest to the poorest, from the most brilliantly intellectual to the most illiterate, kneel in adoration of this Jesus who was crucified in the reign of the second Caesar. Here are two unquestionable facts which demand, as a bare intellectual necessity, a third fact to account for them and make sense of them. There is only one fact which is big enough to do this. The truth is that the resurrection of Jesus Christ from the dead is as well attested by as good evidence as any event in ancient history; and centuries of the severest and most critical investigation have failed to shake it.

CHAPTER V

THE SPIRITUAL BODY

WE CAN now go on with our discussion of the Christian belief in the resurrection of the body. Unless we insist on dismissing the resurrection narratives in the New Testament as the merest fiction, a thing which few competent critical scholars would be prepared to do, there are certain things which these records make quite clear and which will help us, at least a little way, in our search for the truth.

First then, it is clear that the Jesus who showed Himself to the apostles many times after the resurrection was not simply a ghost or disembodied spirit. It is testimony to the honest sincerity of the Gospel narratives that they make no attempt to conceal the fact that this is precisely what the apostles thought He was. They make no secret of their natural terror when He whom they had seen crucified appeared and spoke to them. But Jesus took considerable care to make them realize at once that He was not some kind of shade or wraith, but a whole and complete personality; not something less than they had known before He died, but vastly more. It is equally clear, however, that Jesus did not return to His former physical life on earth. His resurrection was no mere re-animation of the body which died on the cross. It was not a case of putting back into the body something which had escaped in the moment of death— the recharging of a dead battery, so to speak. Such an idea is rejected by Christianity, and it is important to realize that it is rejected not merely because it conflicts with the current ideas of modern science, but because it conflicts with the facts of the Gospel narrative itself. We have only to read the record carefully in order to realize quite clearly that there were marked differences between the body with which Jesus appeared to the apostles after the resurrection and that body which had been nailed to the cross. A great change had come over it. For example, it was no longer subject to the limitations and needs of this present world as it had been before. Jesus could, whenever He willed, conform to those limitations, as He did in the Upper Room and on the lake shore; but He was no longer fast bound by them. We know from experience how the body hampers and constrains the spirit. Our bodies grow weary and hungry; they are never completely under our control or perfectly responsive to our will; they tie us down to the laws of space and time and gravity. From all these earthly limitations the risen body of the Lord was free, and He could now express Himself, not partially and very imperfectly, as we do, but completely, perfectly, as and when and where He willed.

But, although the Lord's body was wonderfully changed by death and resurrection, yet it is equally clear that it had not lost all connection and continuity with that body which had been laid in the tomb. Even though it was with some little difficulty at first, the apostles were able to recognize Jesus and were soon convinced, beyond any doubt, that He was the same person with whom they had lived and worked for the past three years. The precise relation between the body which was laid in Joseph's tomb and that with which Christ appeared after the resurrection, we do not know and do not pretend to know, any more than we know, for example, the precise relation between our own minds and bodies now. A human brain is a material thing, consisting of a few ounces of sticky gray matter which a surgeon can hold in the palm of his hand and on which wonderful and delicate operations can be performed, sometimes with amazing effects upon the personality of the patient. But what is a human mind? What is the precise relation between brain (which is strictly material) and mind (which is strictly immaterial)? We just do not know. All we do know is that in some wonderful and mysterious way they are intimately related and constantly interacting upon each other, so that a blow on the skull or the touch of a scalpel can have the most far-reaching effects upon a person's mind and character. The study of the anatomy of the brain and the practice of brain surgery is producing wonderful results, but we still cannot explain the mysterious relation between the brain and the mind. Even the material particles that form our bodies are constantly wearing out and being replaced, so that the human body is almost completely renewed about every seven years. This means that I, for example, have worn out and discarded no fewer than six bodies in my lifetime, and the body that my friends now see and recognize is not the one I had ten years ago. Yet I can remember things that happened to me thirty years ago, and I am quite sure they happened to me and not to somebody else. Why? Because the thing that persists and lives, surviving all bodily change and decay, is not mere physical continuity, but the unbroken relationship between the personality, which is a spiritual entity, and the medium of its self-expression, which, in this world of time and space, is a certain mass of chemical matter which we call a body. But it is the relation between the two that matters. Thus the recognizable continuity between the body that was nailed to the cross and that which the apostles saw after the resurrection was due, not to physical survival or the re-animation of a corpse, but rather to the fact that what was recognized in each case was the manifestation of one and the same personality. In other words, death and resurrection had effected a wonderful and mysterious change, not in Christ's essential personality, but simply in the medium of its expression and recognition. An illustration may help to make the meaning clearer. The passage of time and the ravages of illness may render a friend, whom we have not seen for twenty years or so, utterly unrecognizable to us physically, so that we should pass him in the street without knowing him. But a few minutes' conversation will establish his identity beyond any doubt; and his personality will break through his completely altered bodily appearance in such a way as to make us wonder why we ever failed to recognize him in the first place.

It may, perhaps, be well to repeat that the foregoing is by no means an attempt at a neat and complete explanation of the mystery of Christ's resurrection from the dead. It is simply a reminder that the mysteries which surround our own existence, of which we are well aware but which we cannot in the least explain, should warn us against the conceit and folly of lightly dismissing as absurd or impossible anything and everything beyond our own present comprehension. Reality is always surrounded by mystery. It is the unreal which is most easily explained. For instance, Euclid defined a straight line as "the shortest distance between two points." When he had said that, he had said all that could be said about a straight line. He had explained it fully and completely. Actually, however, there is no such thing as a straight line. It is an imaginary conception of the human mind. But take something which is unquestionably real, like a bee or a baby, and you can spend a lifetime studying it and know very little about it at the end. If the means of Christ's manifestation of Himself to the apostles after the resurrection had *not* been mysterious, we should have better reason to suspect its reality.

Now it is an essential doctrine of the Christian Faith that the resurrection of Jesus Christ from the dead is the pledge and guarantee of our own. The reason for this, to put it very briefly, is that in the life and personality of Jesus Christ, we see, not only the self-revelation of God in terms of time and space small enough for man to understand, but also the revelation of the nature and character of man as God intends him to be. In this twentieth century it is often difficult to convince people, including many who would call themselves Christians, that Jesus Christ is truly God. But in the first few centuries of the Christian era the difficulty was rather to convince them that He was truly man. That is why the statements of the Christian belief in the Apostles and Nicene creeds insist that Jesus Christ is not only true God but also true man, the archetype and representative of humanity created in the image of God. And so the Christian belief is that, as with Jesus Christ, so also with us, nothing that belongs to the completeness and perfection of our nature and personality will be finally lost through physical death. As we possess the means of self-expression and recognition, in the form of a physical body perfectly and wonderfully adapted to the conditions of this world, so also, in the life of the world to come, we shall possess the means of self-expression and recognition perfectly adapted to the conditions of that life, whatever those conditions may be. As to the exact nature of such means, we cannot speak, because it is entirely outside our present experience. The best St. Paul could do by way of a name for it was to call it a "spiritual body," and we cannot improve on that expression. We believe it will be real—

as real as that with which the risen Christ made Himself known to His disciples. Further than that we cannot go.

And so this article of the Apostles' Creed, "I believe in the resurrection of the body," was deliberately retained in this form, even at the risk of popular misunderstanding and misinterpretation (as much in the first centuries of Christian history as in the twentieth) because it safeguards three important features of Christian belief about eternal life: First, in the Christian belief, eternal life is not a kind of impoverished and ghostly survival of death, like that of the pale shades of the Greek underworld; but life more abundant, complete, and perfect than we know now. Second, it has nothing to do with reincarnation or the re-animation of our physical bodies. (In this context the word "body" signifies, not its physico-chemical constitution, but its relation to a particular personality of whom it is the recognizable expression in time and space. This article thus affirms the Christian belief in the unbroken continuity of personal identity between this life and that of the world to come.) Third, eternal life, for the Christian, means not the swallowing up of his identity in the Being of God, but a perfect relationship with God; a relationship, however, in which I (including all that is meant by "I") shall still be myself, not less but more fully and completely than I am now, and "knowing even as also I am known."

CHAPTER VI

JUDGMENT

IN OUR study of belief in the life of the world
to come we have turned from general considerations
to those particular features which distinguish the
Christian Faith from the doctrines of Greek philosophy or the Wisdom literature of the Jews. One such

feature, as we have seen in the last two chapters, is the doctrine of the resurrection of the body. We must now turn to another strong feature of the Christian belief, namely, its moral content.

In the early instinctive belief in life beyond death, which is found in every race of human beings who have ever inhabited the earth, there is nothing we can clearly recognize as ethical or moral. In other words, the condition of a person's life in the here-after is never supposed to be dependent in any way upon the moral quality of the life he leads in this present world. There is no question of judgment. The teaching of Jesus Christ stands in startling contrast with this, for judgment is its dominant theme. It is to this theme that we must now turn our attention.

But first a much-needed word of caution. The definite and precise information given in the teaching of Jesus is very little, and we must resist the temptation to exaggerate it. We must also remember that the language used by Jesus in speaking of judgment, heaven, and hell was the contemporary language of poetic imagery and symbolism. Here we must be careful to steer a middle course between two common errors. On the one hand, we must not

65

take such language with a literalness it will not bear; and on the other hand, we must remember that the symbolism does, nevertheless, portray an underlying reality and truth. With these precautions in mind, let us see if we can discover the essentials of Christ's teaching on this subject.

First, I think we can say with reasonable certainty that His estimate of the value of human life and personality is always given in terms of eternal life. For Him, the supreme importance of this life is that it is the beginning, for better or for worse, of eternal life, which is not something which only begins after we have passed through physical death, but which we have already begun. This means, for Christ, that every act of moral choice we make is fraught with eternal consequences. Second, there can surely be no doubt (if the Gospels are even an approximate representation of His teaching) that Jesus Himself believed in a final judgment. His many parables of judgment find their climax in the twenty-fifth chapter of the Gospel according to St. Matthew, where Jesus presents, as a sublime finale, a dramatic picture of the judgment of all nations. This has been called "perhaps the most awe-inspiring passage in the literature of the world, as well as the most full of unearthly beauty." [1] The language is highly figurative and full of symbolism and we cannot take it literally: but it clearly affirms and emphasizes the principle of judgment and separation. There is no trace here of universalism. Jesus clearly taught that not one but two possibilities lie open before us—Heaven and Hell. We may accept His teaching, or we may reject it; but there can be little doubt as to what His teaching is. Most of us are quite willing, even eager, to accept the idea of Heaven—at any rate for our loved ones, even if we are not too anxious to get there ourselves yet awhile! And perhaps we take rather too literally the conceptions of Heaven perpetuated in some of our hymns, from which, unfortunately, many people derive the only ideas about Heaven they ever remember. But the doctrine of Hell is difficult, and we tend to do one of two things. Either we dismiss the very idea of Hell as utterly incompatible with the love of God, and say, in effect, "There can't possibly be any such thing. It's just a medieval superstition. God is merciful. He would never condemn any soul to Hell. Everything will be all right in the end." Or else we

[1] *New Commentary* (London: Society for Promoting Christian Knowledge), 196. Article on St. Matthew by P. P. Levertoff and H. L. Goudge, 1932.

may make the opposite mistake of thinking of Hell as an everlasting inferno designed especially for our enemies and the people we dislike most. Is there anyone, I wonder, who has never said to himself in a heated moment, on witnessing some abominable cruelty to a child, for example: "Well, if that swine doesn't suffer in Hell, there's no justice in Heaven!" How many of us could honestly say that we have never felt like that? The fact is that there is, in the very heart of man, a deep-rooted instinct for retribution. But the heart of man is easily swayed by the passions and prejudices of the passing moment. Man's justice is, at best, a very rough justice, based only on half-knowledge and half-ignorance of his fellows. But even man recognizes, instinctively, that good is good and evil is evil and that there is between them a difference deep and dividing, eternally irreconcilable. It is the deliberate refusal to recognize this difference that leads to what Jesus called blasphemy against the Holy Spirit of God; [2] for if we confuse good and evil by turning the light that is in us to darkness, so that finally we cannot tell one from the other, then we have destroyed the very possibility of repentance, which is the

[2] Mark 3:22–30.

68

indispensable condition of forgiveness, and are "guilty of an eternal sin." But, thank God, a man must be very far gone in iniquity before he really fails to recognize the eternal difference between good and evil, right and wrong. And shall the justice of God be less than the justice of man? "Shall not the Judge of all the earth do right?" [3] Yes, He will indeed. And we must try to get our thinking clear about these things because, as we tried to show earlier, the way we think and believe about these things has a profound, even if unconscious, effect upon our daily life and character. Out of our beliefs are born our deeds; out of our deeds we form our habits; out of our habits grows our character; and on our character we build our destiny.

This leads naturally to the third significant thing that Jesus clearly teaches about the judgment of God, namely, that it is not the arbitrary whim or caprice of a moody tyrant. We can gladly and heartily agree with those who say that God does not condemn or send any soul to Hell. In the dramatic picture of the Last Judgment, to which we have already referred,[4] there is one vitally important point, frequently overlooked, which we must point

---

[3] Genesis 18:25.   [4] Matthew 25:31-46.

out because it makes all the difference in the meaning. Jesus presents this famous picture of the Last Judgment under the figure of a shepherd separating the sheep from the goats. But notice that the shepherd, who represents God, does not decide which of the animals shall be the sheep and which shall be the goats. Already, long before they come to him, they *are* either sheep or goats; and all the shepherd does is to separate them *according to what they already are.* In other words, the judgment of God is not in the least comparable with the judgments pronounced in our earthly courts of justice. Such a comparison is, perhaps, almost inevitable; but we must try to get away from it because it only confuses the issue. In our courts of justice the verdict has to depend on evidence which may be false and on the testimony of witnesses who may perjure themselves. And the sentence, at least to some extent, depends on the character and personality of a judge who, however upright he may be, is not omniscient; who must assess the evidence as he hears it and who cannot be entirely free from those passions and prejudices that affect us all. With God the situation is entirely different. At the bar of His justice there is no possibility of error. To Him all

70

hearts are open, all desires are known, and from Him no secrets are hid. God needs no witnesses to testify for any man, for He knows what is in man and is entirely unmoved by passion or prejudice. Above all, and most dreadful of all, God does not pronounce sentence upon us, but allows us to pronounce sentence upon ourselves. That is the most awe-inspiring thing about the love of God—this fearful freedom to choose, which He will not take away from us. The Psalmist realized this profound truth twenty-five centuries ago when he exclaimed, "If thou, Lord, shouldest mark iniquities, O Lord, who shall stand? But there is forgiveness with thee, that thou mayest be feared." [5] This may seem a strange thought, that we should fear (i.e., stand in awe of) God, not because He is sternly just, but because He is merciful; because He respects human personality enough to trust us with choices and decisions of eternal consequence. But the thought is only strange for two reasons. First, because we have an inherent tendency to shirk responsibility and put it onto someone else. (If we can put it onto God, so much the better! But this we cannot do, unless we are prepared to renounce the very thing that makes

[5] Psalms, 130; 3 & 4.

71

us human.) Second, because it is so easy to sentimentalize about the love and fatherhood of God in
such a way as to equate it with the flabby futility of
an overindulgent or emotionally unstable parent
who cannot distinguish between discipline and
cruelty.

The essential truth at the heart of Christ's teaching about the judgment of God is this: So far from
being the arbitrary verdict of a despotic tyrant, it is,
in fact, the eternal fixation of moral character. This,
surely, is what the writer of the Book of the Revelation means in that almost terrifying sentence in the
twenty-second chapter and the eleventh verse.
Almost suddenly, it seems, he drops his imagery
and symbolism and says, in cold and measured
terms: "Let the evildoer still do evil, and the filthy
still be filthy, and the righteous still do right, and
the holy still be holy." [6] This, if we are willing to
ponder its significance, is a sobering thought. But
even if it does no more than help us get away from
the mental image of God as a despotic tyrant, deal-
ing out damnation to some and salvation to others,
as a modern dictator favors his friends and liqui-

[6] Rev; 22:11. (Revised Standard Version)

72

dates his enemies at the whim of the moment, then it will lead us to a better understanding of what the Christian religion means by the judgment of God. It will remind us that, in the thought and teaching of Jesus, eternal life is a matter of *quality* rather than mere quantity. It is not just more life: it is life more abundant. And it is life based on the full recognition of the eternal difference between right and wrong, good and evil.

It can hardly be repeated too often that Christianity, despite the shortcomings and weaknesses of individual Christians, is not interested in the mere prolongation of life regardless of its moral and spiritual quality. The Christian doctrine of judgment satisfies a deep hunger in the human heart. Instinct and reason alike demand the kind of judgment which neither history nor the individual conscience can pronounce. The "verdict of history" has had to be reversed more than once in the light of new knowledge; and the individual conscience is beclouded by ignorance. The only true, eternal and irreversible verdict (and man will be satisfied with nothing less!) is one which is pronounced with total and absolute knowledge of the whole truth. Such knowledge belongs to God alone. That is why the judgment of God, in Christian thought, is called the "last" or "final" judgment.

But we must not let this word "last" mislead us into thinking of the final judgment as if it were a single, sudden, and catastrophic event in the far-distant future. The last scene of a good play would be almost meaningless in isolation from all the acts and scenes and situations which went before it and led up to it. So also the judgment of God is a continuous process, and the "last" judgment is, as it were, the climax which has gradually been made inevitable by all that has gone before. We often use the word "crisis" and speak of the "critical" times through which we are passing. "Crisis" is simply the New Testament Greek word for judgment, and the crises of history are, in a very real sense, manifestations of the judgment of God upon the affairs of men.

But Christian thought has always distinguished two special phases of the judgment of God. One, as we have seen is called the last, or final judgment, which Jesus portrayed under the image of a shepherd separating the sheep from the goats. The other is called the "particular" judgment. One of the few points on which there is almost universal agreement between Christian thinkers of all periods and all communions is that death marks the end of our period of probation and the exercise of our freedom of choice and moral responsibility, and is followed immediately by the particular judgment, i.e., the judgment of the individual soul as distinct from the last or general judgment of all nations. It is in this sense that the very act of dying has, indeed, a fearful finality which Christianity makes no attempt to deny or disguise. It leads to an important question to which we must now turn.

CHAPTER VII

THE INTERMEDIATE STATE

IT IS fairly obvious that most of us, when we come to die, are neither perfectly fit for the immediate presence of God, which is Heaven, nor yet reprobate enough for the absence of God, that "outer darkness" [1] which is Hell. "There is so much good in the worst of us, And so much bad in the best of us. . . ." The truth of those familiar lines is surely beyond question. For the most part, we ordinary mortals are neither pure white nor jet black, but varying shades of gray! It is evident, too, that while some people have both the opportunity and the desire to prepare themselves for death, and to make their peace with God and their fellow men, others, even if they have the desire, are denied the opportunity. Yet the consensus of Christian thought and belief in all ages of the Faith affirms that death is followed immediately by the particular judgment. It seems, therefore, that we are faced with two possibilities. Either the very act of dying, which is nearly always involuntary, and frequently sudden, accidental, and violent, changes us immediately and automatically, from gray to pure white or jet black, so that we are thereby fitted for Heaven or Hell as the case may be; or else there must be some kind of intermediate state of existence intervening between the particular judgment at death and the final judgment. Which of these alternatives commends itself to our reason?

[1] Matthew 8:12; 22:13; 25:30.

77

The old tag—"Speak nothing but good of the dead"—is an excellent precept, provided it is not carried to extremes. But we all know what so often happens in popular sentiment. Bill Jones, alive and well, may have been a very questionable character; but Bill Jones on the day of his funeral is apt to figure as an angel of light! In calmer moments, however, we know quite well that wishing will not make it so. Some kind of intermediate state of life, between death and the final judgment, seems, in fact, to be almost an intellectual necessity; and this is, in reality, what the Christian Church as a whole has believed from the very earliest times. Since the Reformation, however, Christian belief has been divided into three main streams.

It is no part of our present purpose to make a critical comparison of them. We shall try to state, briefly, what they are and concern ourselves chiefly with what they have in common. On the one hand, there is the Roman doctrine of Purgatory and the various religious practices that go with it. The doctrine of Purgatory was made an official dogma of the Roman Communion at the Council of Trent in the sixteenth century. The practices associated with this doctrine, such as the multiplication of masses for

78

the dead, the chantry system, and the sale of pardons and indulgences were, of course, among the principal causes of the Reformation. On the other hand, there is (or was, for it is now largely discarded even by the communions that still bear his name) the doctrine of John Calvin, who taught that God, from the beginning, had predestinated a fixed number of souls for eternal salvation and the rest for eternal damnation, and that there was nothing anybody could do about it. The strain of Calvinism, however, is not entirely extinct, even in the Anglican Communion, and the more distinctly "Evangelical" tradition, with its strong emphasis on the doctrine of Justification by Faith, is content to think of the faithful departed as being immediately "in joy and felicity" as soon as they are "delivered from the burden of the flesh." [2] On this, as on so many other questions, the Anglican Communion, as a whole, stands midway between Rome and Geneva. With an intellectual and spiritual humility born of sound learning and true wisdom, she leaves room on this question both for the characteristically "Evangelical" view mentioned above and also for the ancient traditional belief in an intermediate state of growth

[2] Order for the Burial of the Dead, *The Book of Common Prayer.*

and development between physical death and the general resurrection "at the last day."

It is this ancient belief in an intermediate state, which has been held by Christians from the very earliest times, that we must now consider. What happens to the soul on its separation from the body by physical death? What happened to the soul of Jesus between the moment of his death on Good Friday afternoon and His resurrection in the early hours of the first day of the week? Just before He died Jesus said to the penitent thief, "Today shalt thou be with me in paradise." [3] On his first appearance to the women in the garden after the resurrection He said, "Touch me not; for I am not yet ascended to my Father." [4] According to the gospel narrative it was forty days after his resurrection that He ascended into Heaven. The only direct clue to the answer to our question which is given in Holy Scripture is that of St. Peter in his First Epistle. In the third chapter and the eighteenth verse, he writes, "Christ . . . being put to death in the flesh but made alive in the spirit [i.e., His human spirit] in which also he went and preached unto the spirits in prison. . . ." [5] And in the fourth chapter and the

[3] Luke 23:43.   [4] John 20:17.   [5] Revised Standard Version.

80

sixth verse: "For this is why the gospel was preached even unto the dead, that though judged in the flesh like men, they might live in the spirit like God." [5] If these two passages are taken together, as they must be, they leave no reasonable doubt as to their author's meaning, namely that Jesus went to the "abode of departed spirits" and preached the word of salvation to them also. This is the truth embodied in the clause "He descended into Hell" in the Apostles' Creed.

Here we must pause to put in a much-needed word of explanation. We must be clear, at the outset, that the word "hell" in this clause has nothing whatever to do with everlasting torment, damnation, or hell-fire. It is a translation, not of Gehenna, the place of torment, but of Hades, the abode of departed spirits. It is an old English word derived from the Anglo-Saxon verb *helen* which means to cover, to conceal, to hide. Even to this day in certain parts of England, the men whose trade is to make and repair thatched roofs, are called *heliers*. And so this clause in the creed means that between his death and resurrection Jesus went to the abode of departed spirits, the hidden, unseen world; and thus consecrated and sanctified with His own presence, not only this earthly life, but also that state of life into which we must all pass at death. If we accept the Christian belief that Christ was, and is, truly man and that He really died, then it is not unreasonable to believe that He entered fully and completely into human experience and shared man's condition after death no less than in His life on earth. This much we can say quite positively, that whatever condition or experience awaits us after death, it is one which Christ Himself has shared. Here too He can say with authority and power, "It is I; be not afraid. Follow me."

As to the conditions of life in this intermediate state, or "place of waiting" as it is sometimes called, the only person who could claim to know seems to be disappointingly reticent. There is so much we long to know that He does not tell us. And we wonder why. Might not the answer be found in those words which, according to St. John, Jesus spoke to the apostles just before he died? "I have yet many things to say unto you, but ye cannot bear them now." [6] To describe "the things eternal" to us, who are at present creatures of time and space, would be like trying to describe the glowing colors of a glo-

[6] John 16:12.

rious sunset to a man born blind. But that does not make the sunset any the less real or beautiful. Could you begin to describe, in written words to a man deaf from birth, the sound of a violin in the hands of Fritz Kreisler? It is well for us to remember that the fact that we may be deaf and blind to the realities of eternal life is no proof that they have no existence. In this respect we have to exercise precisely the same kind of faith that a blind man puts in a sighted person who leads him across a busy street.

It is worth noting, in passing, that although the man must exercise faith in his guide because he is blind, yet the faith he exercises is not blind faith. It is based upon reason. It is a rational act of confidence in human character, based on knowledge and experience but going trustfully beyond them. We have tried to show that the Christian's belief in eternal life is faith of this kind; not blind, irrational credulity based on ignorance, but reasonable confidence, a rational act of trust in a Person, based on knowledge of His life and character. And so, although Jesus gives us none of those details about life after death which most of us long to know, He has at least shown us that the condition of those whom we call "the faithful departed" is not that of a deep and dreamless sleep of passive unconsciousness, but of gradual and continual growth and development toward that perfection which will fit them for the immediate presence of God, which is Heaven. Whether or not this process of purification involves pain is a matter of opinion. Some forms of purification in this life are painful, both bodily and spiritually, and it is not unreasonable to suppose that the gradual cleansing away of those stains which have soiled the soul on its journey through life may be painful too. But we do not know. In the very nature of the case we cannot know and it is futile to dogmatize about it. All that St. Augustine would say was that such an idea was "not incredible," and we may, perhaps, be inclined to agree with him.

What then can we say, with reasonable confidence and the support of the best Christian thought in all ages, of those whom we love but now no longer see? If, as we hope and believe, they have been acquitted in the particular judgment, then we can be sure of this at least: that although they may not yet have reached that absolute purity and perfection which alone will fit them for the immediate presence of God, which is Heaven, yet they are safe from that eternal banishment from His presence which is Hell, and are living and growing in the love and service of God, and in the nearer presence of Jesus Christ.

CHAPTER VIII

HEAVEN AND HELL

W<small>E HAVE</small> already seen, in the chapter on
judgment, that according to the clear teaching of
Jesus Christ, not one but two possibilities lie before
us as morally responsible human beings endowed
with the Godlike power of free will. In the lan-

guage of Christian theology, these two possibilities are called Heaven and Hell.

It is probably unnecessary to emphasize the fact that Christianity does not conceive of either Heaven or Hell as places with a geographical location. The golden streets and harps and halos of Heaven, no less than the ever-burning fires and fumes of Hell, are symbols which bear testimony to the poverty of human thought and language to conceive or express these tremendous realities. It is easy to make fun of them and there are innumerable funny stories about them, partly because so many people just do not believe in the existence of either Heaven or Hell, and partly because a destiny beyond death, which does not involve either time or space, is so difficult to conceive. We live in a materialistic age which equates reality with tangibility; an age which seems to value only that which may be seen and handled. The intangibles, the things of the spirit that are not seen and cannot be handled, are apt to be regarded as unreal, fanciful imaginings. Until they begin to hurt! And then we make the discovery that a broken heart, for example, can hurt even more than a diseased heart. Yet while a diseased heart is a solid, material thing which can be seen and handled, and on which a surgeon can operate, a "broken heart" is nothing but a figure of speech, a symbol which cannot be taken at all literally and which has no reference to time or space. When we use the expression "a broken heart," we do not mean that the mass of muscle and tissue which pumps blood through our arteries has been fractured, even though that is the literal significance of the words. Actually we mean something quite different. We mean a condition of pain which is not bodily, suffering which is not physical, and distress which no material, tangible things (like dressings or drugs) can affect in the slightest degree. It would be almost impossible to describe in words just what this familiar expression really does mean; and even the most eloquent and accurate description would have but little meaning for one whose life had always been happy and pleasant and who was not acquainted with grief. But we use the phrase "a broken heart" because it is a convenient and brief figure of speech which does convey at least some part of the unquestionable reality of human experience which it symbolizes.

In the same way, the words Heaven and Hell have passed into our common everyday speech as symbols of equally vivid realities of human experience. In spite of the use of "Heaven" to denote a place where one eats hamburgers, and "Hell" as a mere expletive of annoyance, we still know approximately what these words are intended to convey and that one has a connotation of pleasure, the other of pain. But the more accurately we use these words to symbolize the spiritual realities of supreme happiness or unmitigated misery, the more we realize that they have practically no reference to time, space, or matter. It is another fact of common experience that it is precisely when we are supremely happy, or else unutterably miserable, that we are *least* conscious of our physical surroundings or the the passage of time; and it is not until the physical or the temporal intrudes itself upon our awareness, by the opening of a door, for instance, or the striking of a clock, that we "come back to earth," as we say in a phrase which contains more truth than we realize.

Let us realize, then, that Heaven and Hell mean states of being, conditions of existence which, even in this present life, can have very little reference to time and space. The important thing is to recognize quite clearly that spiritual realities are none the less real and actual because they are spiritual. The thing that makes this difficult to realize is that mysterious but intimate relationship between the spirit and the body, which we have already discussed. Happiness, misery, sorrow, fear, disappointment, hope, joy, or anxiety can certainly affect our material bodies. Tears, blushes, and stomach ulcers are familiar examples. On the other hand, bodily pain or wretched physical conditions can certainly affect the spirit and make the achievement of joy and happiness much more difficult. *But not impossible.* That is important. Those who spend a great deal of time among people who are in bodily pain or miserable living conditions, are constantly amazed at the ability of the human spirit to triumph over the most appalling physical and material circumstances, and achieve a state of peaceful happiness and calm serenity seldom seen in the lives of those whose lot is cast in pleasant places. The fact is that happiness and misery, joy and sorrow, love and hate, are spiritual realities which are fundamentally independent, even in this present life, of time, place, and matter. One man may be young, healthy and wealthy, and yet miserably unhappy to the point of black despair. Another may be old, sick and poverty-stricken, and yet possessed of a serene happiness which he would not exchange for the other man's youth, health, or wealth. This is neither fanciful imagining nor wishful thinking. The present writer has seen it too often to have the least remaining doubt about its truth.

If we set this truth alongside some of the conclusions we have reached earlier, we shall see, perhaps, where they will lead us. As we tried to show in Chapter II, there is not the slightest logical or demonstrable reason to assume that the destruction of the physical body by death necessarily involves the annihilation of the spiritual personality, which may perfectly well go on living a life of its own. Christians and many others believe that it does. But because a disembodied spirit is something less than a whole and complete person, the Christian Faith teaches that the spirit is re-equipped, or, as St. Paul expresses it, "reclothed" with a new medium of self-expression and recognition which is as perfectly adapted to the conditions of life after death as the physical body is to this present life on earth. It is obvious that the physical body, wonderful as it is, hinders and restrains the spirit because it is fast bound within the limits of time and space and matter. But, even while it is still wedded so intimately

91

to the body, the human spirit can, and does, achieve a great measure of independence of the body's condition and circumstances. When that independence is made complete and absolute by the death of the body, it is neither unreasonable nor illogical to expect that the spiritual experiences of the soul (spirit, ego, self, personality, or whatever name we give it) will be even more, rather than less, real. The vital question is: Will those experiences be pleasant or painful, happy or miserable, beautiful or ugly? In a word—Heaven or Hell? What is the deciding factor?

In the chapter on judgment, we saw that a distinguishing feature of the Christian doctrine of eternal life is its moral content. It involves considerations of right and wrong, good and evil, sin and righteousness. And here we must put in a brief word of caution about some popular but mistaken ideas. How many of us were told, when we were young children, that if we were good we would go to Heaven with the implication, understood if not expressed, that if we were bad we would go to Hell! This put Heaven and Hell in the same categories as fairies and bogeymen, which are strictly for children and a few weak-minded adults. On the other hand, there are many who think of Heaven as the just reward of good deeds done in this world and of Hell as the equally just punishment for evil deeds; and that their eternal destiny will depend on whether the balance, at the closing of the books, is on the debit or credit side of the ledger. Two generations ago, Hell-fire and damnation was the great theme of pulpit oratory. And even today there are millions who would live in deadly fear of Hell, if it were not for the somewhat mechanical means which, they believe, will enable them to escape it by the performance, often perfunctory, of certain prescribed religious exercises. Religion of this kind is very apt to become little more than a kind of spiritual fire insurance. The man who is "righteous" because he hopes thereby to earn an eternity of bliss, or because he is terrified of Hell, is no better morally and spiritually than the man who gives a million dollars to a good cause for the sake of the publicity, or the man who conducts his business within the law because he is terrified of prison.

What then is the true relation between good and evil and Heaven and Hell? We shall find the answer, I believe, in the remarkable fact (which often passes unnoticed) that in all the teaching, sermons, and parables recorded in the gospels, Jesus never once urged anyone to be good. He seems to have avoided using the word quite deliberately, for it is not merely a matter of translation. And on the one recorded occasion when someone called Him good, He disapproved of it strongly. "Why callest thou me good?" He asked the young man. "None is good, save one, that is, God."[1] Instead, He was constantly urging people, by precept and example, to learn to love. Of the notorious prostitute who came and wept at His feet, He said, "Her sins, which are many, are forgiven; for she loved much." [2] Above all He urges love towards God, and His own definition of Heaven is the supreme joy of seeing and knowing God, because to know Him is to love Him.

The point is that we do not willingly hurt those whom we love. From time to time we may do so, through weakness or ignorance; but after we have done it we are sorry. So also the man who loves God will strive to do what pleases God and to avoid what offends—not in the hope of reward or in fear of punishment, but for precisely the same reason as a man will try to do what will give happiness and avoid what will give pain to the wife he loves; just

[1] Luke 18:19.   [2] Luke 7:47.

because he loves her. No other motive is necesary
or even possible. If, through weakness or ignorance,
he does cause her pain, then he will be sorry, he
will apologize and try to make amends. And his only
"reward" will be the opportunity and the ability to
love her more. So, again, it is with the man who
loves God. His great reward will be to see and know
God and thus to have the supreme joy of loving Him
perfectly and forever. Such a reward as this has no
attraction whatever for the man who does not love
God, and it would certainly not be a strong enough
motive to make him renounce the pleasures of sin!
The Christian's hope of Heaven, therefore, is not in
the least like that of a man who strives to please the
president of his firm (whom he may loathe person-
ally) in the hope of winning promotion. The
Christian's hope of immortality is the hope of one
who, having experienced a little of what it means
to love—and yet realizes how human love in this
world is spoiled by jealousy and possessiveness—
longs to be able to love perfectly.

But what shall we say about Hell? Perhaps we
can laugh at that "mixture of buffoonery and sav-
agery" which constituted the medieval idea of Hell,
with its fire and flames and shrieks of agony. Per-

haps we can afford to make jokes and tell funny stories about it, because we feel that it has no reality. But what of the fires of hatred, greed and envy, malice and jealousy that burn so insatiably in the human heart? We all know how real they are, and most of us have felt at least a touch of the pain they cause; and if, in the words of Jesus, "Their worm dieth not [the worm of gnawing desire increasingly incapable of satisfaction] and their fire is not quenched" [3]—the fire of burning lust or hate or jealousy—then that is Hell even worse and far more real than Dante's wildest dreams. Nor do we have to wait for death before we feel a foretaste of it. We can hardly afford to laugh at that, for Hell is as real as man's ugliest passions, and Heaven as his purest love.

It has been well said that the doctrine of Hell is the greatest compliment ever paid to mankind, for it means that our freedom is absolute. It means that it is within our power, if we choose, even to reject the Kingdom of Heaven. Just as the worship of God on earth can, and does, become utterly meaningless, boring and dull to the person who has so fashioned his life that God has no place in it, so also the eternal

[3] Mark 9:44.

96

worship and adoration of Heaven would be, for the soul that had finally rejected God, just plain Hell! Whether any soul has, in fact, ever made that final great refusal we do not know. But if Hell is not at least a possibility, then human free will is a pathetic illusion. If man is really free, then he must be free to choose, not only where he will spend a two-week summer vacation, but whether he will spend eternity with God, which is Heaven, or without Him, which is Hell. It is true, as we have readily admitted, that the language of Jesus is not to be taken literally (any more than the phrase "a broken heart"), yet it warns us solemnly, clearly and quite unmistakably of a possibility so inexpressibly awful that God Himself, in the person of Jesus Christ "came down from heaven, And was incarnate by the Holy Ghost of the Virgin Mary, And was made man" [4] just to make it possible for us to escape such a fate. Few would deny that it must certainly be the will and deep desire of God that all men should be saved and come to the knowledge of the truth.[5] But it seems equally true from the teaching of the Gospel that God will not save them against their will. God Himself could not have given man free will which is not really free, for God

[4] Nicene Creed. [5] I Timothy 2:4.

97

cannot contradict Himself or do what is contrary to
His own nature. Every person, therefore, who possesses the divine attribute of free will and moral
choice, has with it, of necessity, at least the possibility of final disobedience and impenitence. It is a
fearful possibility which Christ bids us contemplate,
not for others, but for ourselves.

CHAPTER IX

THE COMMUNION OF SAINTS

CHRISTIAN history knows of no time when Christians did not pray for the departed, and it is only since the Reformation that there have been two opinions about it. The tragedy of any reformation is that, in gathering up the tares, we are apt to uproot some of the wheat with them. This is what happened in the sixteenth century with the practice of prayer for the departed. In a natural, but violent, reaction against the scandalous sale of pardons and indulgences in connection with the Roman doctrine of Purgatory, many Christians went to the other extreme and abandoned entirely the practice of prayer for the departed. For example, in the English Book of Common Prayer of 1552, which was compiled under strong continental influence, all prayers for the departed were removed, and no part of the order for the Burial of the Dead was allowed to be read in the church. The body had to be taken straight to the grave! Happily, however, wiser counsels prevailed in later revisions and today, the commemoration of the faithful departed finds its place in the very heart and center of the liturgy of the Episcopal Church.

Many Christian people, however, are still dubious, if not definitely against the practice of praying for the departed. It is hard to see how the great Christian doctrine of the Communion of Saints can have any real meaning for them because, if that Communion means anything at all, it must include, at least, that fellowship of mutual prayer and intercession which is not only the hallmark of any Christian communion here on earth, but also the very breath of its life. If we believe in prayer at all, and if we pray for our loved ones while they are in this world, then why should we abandon them, slam the door behind them, so to speak, at the moment of physical death? The only justification for doing so is the belief that, at the moment of death, their eternal destiny is fixed forever and that any further prayers for them are of no avail. If any man chooses to believe that, we cannot question his right to do so.

But if, as we tried to show in Chapter VII, it seems more reasonable to accept the ancient belief in an intermediate state of life between death and the final judgment, then the case is altered. While our loved ones were with us here on earth, we had other opportunities, whether we used them or not, to help them in other ways besides praying for them. And if we did pray for them, we surely prayed not only for their bodily and material welfare, but for their spiritual welfare too. Now that they have passed within the veil, the least (and, incidentally, the most) we can do for them is to remember them faithfully and regularly in our prayers. If the Christian hope of eternal life is anywhere near the truth, we may be quite sure that they, in the nearer presence of Christ, have not ceased to pray for us. The writer of the Epistle to the Hebrews pictures them as the crowd in the stands of a great arena [1] watching and encouraging the efforts of the young athletes. So long as we remember that the true object of all Christian prayer is not that God's will may be changed, but that it may be done, and His purpose for creation find its perfect fulfilment, then prayer for the faithful departed can do nothing but good for those who pray as well as for those in whose behalf we pray. But human memory is short and though we may deny it fervently at the time of bereavement, we have a wonderful capacity to forget. Time blurs the sharpest image and dulls the edge of the keenest grief. We may be grateful that it is so, otherwise life would become intolerable. But faithful prayer for our loved ones who have gone before translates remembrance from words into positive activity, and sentiment and sorrow into spiritual power. The sense of nearness and unbroken fellowship that such prayer brings is the reality at the heart of the doctrine of the Communion of Saints;

[1] Hebrews 12:1.

102

but it is something which must be discovered by personal practice and experience, rather than by logical argument.

We must be careful, however, to make a clear distinction between praying to God in behalf of our departed loved ones and invoking the prayers of the saints in behalf of ourselves. Here again the practice of Christians is divided into three main streams. The Roman Church makes a definite distinction between the formally canonized saints, who are regarded as having already attained to Heaven, and the faithful departed in general who are regarded as being in Purgatory. It is the practice of Roman Catholic Christians to invoke the prayers of the saints for benefits desired (often particular saints by name for particular benefits) and to pray, especially at Mass, for those who are in Purgatory. The Eastern Orthodox Church, on the other hand, makes no such clear and sharp distinction, and an Eastern Christian would see nothing incongruous in praying to God for the Blessed Virgin and asking his own dead mother to pray for him. Protestantism, on the whole, has almost entirely abandoned both the invocation of saints and prayer for the departed. The latter finds its recognized place in the Order for Holy

Communion in the Episcopal Church, but is not otherwise popularly practiced. And while many fraternal organizations hold memorial services, these, in the present writer's experience, rarely include prayers for the souls of the departed.

It is no part of our purpose to argue the relative merits and demerits of these three positions. It is evident that all three are attended with spiritual dangers. While both the Roman and Eastern customs are very apt to lead to gross superstition and an undignified "canvassing" of the saints for favors, the Protestant position, on the other hand, leaves an empty blank from the moment of physical death and forfeits that deep sense of the Church as the community and fellowship of all faithful people, living and departed alike, in the mystical body of Christ. This is a serious loss which is undoubtedly a great source of weakness to the Protestant communions today. Not only does it cut us off from the future by making physical death the end of any conceivable kind of communion and fellowship for which the heart of man so desperately yearns, and thereby drives so many to seek satisfaction in grave-worship and the baser forms of spiritualism, but also it cuts us off from our glorious past by destroying our sense of continuity with those who were the chosen vessels of God's grace, and lights of the world in their several generations.

How then are we to repair the loss without incurring the attendant dangers of superstition? The fact is that most of the objections raised against prayer on behalf of the faithful departed are really objections against prayer itself. But if we do believe in prayer, and if we also believe that "the souls of the righteous are in the hand of God" then it surely cannot be wrong for us to make known to God in prayer the hopes and desires for them that we carry in our hearts.

"We cannot in any case go wrong if we ask, on behalf of those who have passed beyond the grave and gate of death, for those things which St. Paul asked on behalf of his converts, namely, that God would grant unto them, according to the riches of His glory, to be strengthened with might by His Spirit in the inward man; that Christ may increasingly dwell in their hearts by faith: and that they, in whatever region of being they now are, may be rooted and grounded in love, and be strong to comprehend with all saints what is the breadth and length and depth and height, and to know the love of Christ which passeth knowledge, and to be filled with all the fullness of God." [2]

[2] A. E. J. Rawlinson, "The Communion of Saints," *The Meaning of the Creed* (London: Society for Promoting Christian Knowledge).

The practice of such prayer as this will not fail to bring its own reward in a deeper understanding of the meaning and the power of the Communion of Saints as an unbroken fellowship of mutual prayer which brings both us and our departed loved ones nearer together by bringing us both nearer to Christ.

CHAPTER X

CONCLUSION

IN THE first chapter we said that firm belief in the Christian doctrine of eternal life makes a difference to life and behavior in this present world, and we may now, by way of conclusion, try to see what kind of difference it makes. In the first place

107

let us be clear that the pain of parting with those we love is no less sharp for the Christian believer than for anyone else. There is a sense in which the very measure of our love is our capacity to suffer. The true Christian is a stark realist and he, more than the non-Christian, realizes very clearly the awful finality of death, because it is the end of our life's probation. It is true that death can come, and often does, thank God, as a friend to be welcomed rather than an enemy to be feared. But it is nevertheles "the wages of sin," the dividing asunder of the soul from that now lifeless body which has meant so much to us. To the Christian who understands his faith, death is not simply "the gateway to life" or "the end of life's fitful fever." It is the inescapable consequence of human sin standing under the eternal judgment of Almighty God. That is why he cannot approve the present tendency, at funeral services for example, to disguise, or to refuse to face, the fact of death. Of course it is kind and right to make things as easy and as comforting as possible for the bereaved at such a time. But it is futile, and rather pathetic, to try to deceive ourselves. Not all the "cheerful" hymns, masses of flowers, eloquent eulogies or misuse of liturgical colors can turn a funeral into a wedding.

If death is *not* the final end of a human life, then the burial of the dead is an even more solemn and awe-inspiring occasion than if it were. And for this reason. If we could be absolutely sure, beyond any shadow of doubt, that bodily death is the final end of a human life and personality, and that beyond death there is nothing at all—the complete and utter nothingness of non-being—then we could be equally sure of something else. We could be sure, for example, that our sorrow at parting with our loved ones was sorrow entirely for ourselves: self-pity at our own irreparable loss by their departure, mingled, perhaps, with remorse for what more we might have been to them while they were still with us. But at the same time we would be comforted by the sure and certain knowledge that they, at any rate, were not sharing our sorrow; that they were beyond all feeling and untroubled by memories or regrets, because, while these things can haunt and torture us in every waking hour, the beloved dead are beyond them all, for they have ceased to be. They are not. We could be quite sure too (still assuming, for the moment, that death really is the end) that while we may be sorrowful at the thought of our own inevitable parting with life and those we love, yet at least we have nothing to fear, no doubts, questions or fearful forebodings; for beyond the closing of our eyes in the deep and dreamless sleep of death, there is no awakening. There is nothing.

But this is the very thing of which we can *not* be sure! It is precisely this uncertainty which gives to the phenomenon of death its awe and mystery, and invests it not only with sorrow (parting which does not involve death can cause deep sorrow) but also with fear, the haunting fear of the unknown. This is the reason why, from the earliest moments of his awareness of himself as a self-conscious personality, man has surrounded the mystery of death with dramatic solemnities, ritual, and ceremonial. Down the ages these customs have varied a little in details, yet, after thousands of years of cultural development they show no signs of disappearing. There are very few, even of the most blatantly irreligious, who direct that their bodies be disposed of with no kind of ritual or ceremonial at all, even though what they do direct may be something entirely pagan. This persistent custom of investing death and burial with solemn symbolism and ceremonial is testimony to man's sheer inability to accept the fact of bodily death as the final end of human life, and leave it at

110

that. It is evidence of his instinctive refusal to believe that human personality has no other end, no higher destiny, than dissolution into non-existence. And hence the hopes and fears, the doubts and ceaseless wonderings, the dreams and aspirations that haunt our hearts as if we were exiles from a native land of which we have no clear recollections, but only vague and fleeting memories which, nevertheless, can fill our very souls with unutterable longing and aching nostalgia.

And so, for the Christian who stands at the open grave of a loved one, the source of strength and consolation lies neither in a stoic determination to forget the past and face the future with a stiff upper lip, nor, on the other hand, in the fetishes of graveworship. It is to be found in the deep and strong conviction that, although we must bear in our hearts the pain of parting and of loneliness, which is the price of love, yet that pain is ours and ours alone, and is not shared by the beloved dead. But—and this is the point—*not* because they are dead, swallowed up in the dark oblivion of eternal annihilation, but because, in the nearer presence of Christ, they are living and growing towards that perfection which will fit them for the high destiny of the pure in heart,

which is to see God. Unless our love has become
entirely self-regarding, we can rejoice in this conviction even in the midst of our sorrow and loneliness.

Another effect of Christian belief in eternal life
is to be found in our attitude towards inevitably approaching death, for ourselves as well as those we
love. There is a well-known petition in the Litany
in which we pray that God will deliver us from "sudden death." This does not mean death by sudden,
unexpected accident, or dropping dead in our tracks
from unsuspected heart disease. It is a prayer that
God may deliver us from a death which, whether it
comes slowly or quickly, early or late, finds us unprepared. It is a commonplace of conversation on
this point to remark that it must be rather a wonderful thing to die in one's sleep, quite peacefully and
without being aware of it. And when we see what
fearful suffering can afflict the human body in linger-
ing illness, it is no more than natural that we should
cherish the hope that when our time comes to die,
we may be allowed, in the words of Keats, "to cease
upon the midnight, with no pain." But the Christian
who believes that "It is appointed unto men once to

112

die, but after this the judgment," [1] will not wish to be deprived, in his last hours, of the opportunity to make the preparations appropriate to the occasion, because he knows that acquittal in the judgment is not for those who have never sinned, but for those whose sins have been truly repented and forgiven.

In view of this we may well ask whether, after all, it is really kind to try to deceive a person who is dying into thinking he is getting well and to dissuade him from even thinking about death. Is this not substituting sentiment for faith and arrogating to ourselves the right of judgment which belongs to God? It is God's judgment he has to face, not ours! It is easy and comforting to assume, without thinking about it too closely, that somehow all will be well; but is it really the patient's feelings we are considering—or our own? It is certainly much easier to do nothing about it and just hope for the best. The reasons given by doctors and others in defense of the "white lies" of the sickroom have a good deal of sound practical psychology behind them; but, apart from the fact that a sick person will clutch eagerly at any hope, one wonders how often the

[1] Hebrews 9:27.

113

patient is really deceived by them. In any case there usually comes a point when the facts have to be faced, and it is a grave responsibility deliberately to allow a soul to launch out into eternity without the opportunity to face them.

These are essentially practical problems about which we have to make decisions, even if we make them by default. If eternal life is a reality, then the preparation we make for it is at least as important as the legal document by which we dispose of our worldly goods, and the sometimes very elaborate directions given for the funeral and the disposal of the body. But the Christian who follows the wise advice, "Repent one day before you die," will never be unprepared because, not knowing when that day will dawn, he will try to end every day in charity with all men and at peace with God.

Perspective is as important in life as it is in art, and the man who sees his life against the background of eternity is more likely to see life in the round and to see it whole. To such a man, this life will not be less, but vastly more, important and worth while, because it is the first stage of his journey, the stage in which the direction of all the rest will be set; either toward, or else away from, his

114

high destiny as a human personality created in the image and for the friendship of God. This is the destiny in which the hopes that haunt man's heart, the dreams that fill his soul, and the soaring search for truth that has driven his mind from ocean depths to starry heights, will find their full, complete, and perfect satisfaction.

Hancock, Harry N.
And after this? an
interpretation of the
Christian belief in life
after death